Presented To

_____

From

_____

Date

_____

PREFACE

The story of Christmas has been told in many different ways, but its underlying meaning remains the same. It is truly a celebration of the birth of a very special child. For generations Christians have recognized this event as one of the cornerstones of their faith. Each year it provides us with a time for reflection and serves as a reminder of the joyous miracle that all children are.

As a child I had always loved Christmas and as a grown-up child I love it even more! Every year during this season my thoughts frequently travel back to the time of that starry night when Christ was born. In fact, this book is a result of one of my many excursions into the memory of that wonderful evening.

It was on a cold December day in 1993 while I was attempting to return home from an artist-in-school residency where I had been working with elementary students all day. I had a long way to get home and the winter weather was getting bad. It was snowing heavily and I had barely made it to a truck stop alongside the interstate. The roads were closed and there was nowhere to go for lodging. The truck stop was filled with disgruntled travelers and there was really no place to sit or stand. So, I chose to wait in my van. I had a sleeping bag for warmth and some snacks to munch on in my emergency kit.

That's when I began to think of how Mary and Joseph must have traveled a great distance and how they too looked for a place to rest. To pass the time I began to write down these thoughts and somehow the story came out in the form of a poem. Earlier that day I had read *A Visit From St. Nicholas* by Clement Clarke Moore to a group of grade school children and perhaps that is why I had that particular rhyming scheme in my head. The next morning the roads were opened and I returned home.

Since that time, I've shared my poem at several Christmas church services and have always had such a wonderful response as well as encouragement to have it published so that others might enjoy its message. With the talents and determination of my wife, Tammy, that has happened. We decided that this book should also serve an objective that reflects the spirit of that timeless tale. That is why we've chosen to have the proceeds from this endeavor go to benefit the Children's Home Society of South Dakota.

This book embodies the efforts of many individuals and organizations who share in that common spirit that has echoed through the ages since the first Christmas so long ago. It is a spirit of love, of giving, of serving, and of hope for the future of our children – of all God's children. I feel very blessed to have so many friends who believe in this book's message as well as its purpose. I am grateful to you all!

Merry Christmas!

- Tom Roberts

Tom Roberts
2010

'Twas The Night Before Christ
Text Copyright © 2002 by Tom Roberts
Illustrations Copyright © 2002 by Steve Hoffman
Printed in the U.S.A. All rights reserved.

Designed by Hoffman Graphic Design
6601 West Strabane Trail
Sioux Falls, SD 57106
Text set in New Century Schoolbook

Printed by Sisson Printing, Inc.
3500 South Duluth Avenue
Sioux Falls, SD 57105
Job # 104445
Press Date: June 2010

ISBN 0-9723-8681-5

'Twas the night before Christ,
and all through the land,
not a creature was stirring,
except two, a woman and a man.

They were tired and hungry
from traveling all day,
and they searched for a place
that would welcome their stay.

But the inns were all full
in the Bethlehem town,
so they went to a stable
and laid themselves down.

Now, the woman, named Mary
was soon to have a child,
and her loving husband, Joseph
looked at her and smiled.

Though weary and worn,
they held each other tight,
while a bright shiny star
up above filled the night.

And there in the hay
on that first Christmas morn,
a baby boy-child, a savior,
Jesus Christ was born!

His eyes how they sparkled,
his face all aglow
and the goodness of God
showed from head to toe.

The sky filled with angels,
and they sang with great joy!
"Hosannah, Glory to God!"
was their song for this boy.

The shepherds in the fields
when they saw this display,
rushed to the Bethlehem stable
where the son of God lay.

The brilliant light overhead
guided people from afar,
to find this joyous miracle
beneath the Christmas star.

Oh, and Mary and Joseph
were as proud as could be
of the little baby Jesus
and their happy family.

For they knew that the world
would be changed forever more
by that tiny blessed infant –
a child of God that Mary bore.

And ever since that time
of the very first Christmas
we've continued to celebrate
the spirit of the Lord Jesus.

With songs and music
and gifts from the heart
with friendship and kindness
and lots of love to impart.

With a smile on our lips
and a gleam in our eyes
the voices of the world
all join in reprise –

Merry Christmas Christians!
To each and every one!
Rejoice in the Lord Jesus!
God's very *special* Son!

THE
BEGINNING

All proceeds from this book are being donated to:

CHILDREN'S HOME SOCIETY

With a history spanning more than a century, Children's Home Society (CHS) is the oldest human service agency in South Dakota. Pioneer child advocates Elizabeth and William Sherrard moved to South Dakota in 1890, and soon became determined to help the growing number of abused and abandoned children in the region. By welcoming those first children into their own home in 1893, Children's Home Society was born. The Sherrards were also instrumental in writing the first child protection laws for the state of South Dakota.

In 1902, construction was completed on the CHS orphanage at 10th & Cliff Avenue in Sioux Falls, and it provided refuge for thousands of children for nearly seventy years. Children's Home served as South Dakota's principal orphanage until the late 1960's when foster care was introduced and became the preferred method of caring for children in crisis.

Since the early 1970's, Children's Home Society has provided a home, school, and therapy for children, ages 4-13, with emotional and behavioral problems. Most are victims of extreme abuse and neglect.

Long regarded as a state leader that champions the welfare of children, Children's Home Society's mission continues—to protect, support, and enhance the lives of children and families. Services are provided through Black Hills Children's Home, just southwest of Rapid City; Sioux Falls Children's Home in Sioux Falls; and Children's Inn in Sioux Falls.

An agency proud of its Christian heritage, the wish of Children's Home Society continues to reflect both the vision of William and Elizabeth Sherrard, as well as the hope of Mary and Joseph—that every child born into this world would be surrounded by love, and be provided the guidance and opportunity to reach their God-given potential.

For more information, visit our web site at: www.chssd.org or call: (605)334-6004.

TOM ROBERTS
Author

Tom Roberts is originally from the Ipswich/Aberdeen area of South Dakota, but he and his wife, Tammy, have lived in Sioux Falls since 1979. In addition to being a writer and storyteller, Tom has performed and taught theatre professionally throughout South Dakota, the Midwest and over-seas since 1983. He also has had extensive experience as commercial talent for numerous TV and radio ads. In 2009 he joined the Children's Home Society of South Dakota as their Event Coordinator.

In February of 1999, Tom was recognized for his talents and contributions to arts education by the Sioux Falls Mayor's Office and Sioux Empire Arts Council when he was chosen to be the recipient of their first annual Outstanding Artist Award.

In the Fall of 1999, Tom's work as an actor and volunteer were featured in a book published by the Lessons In Leadership foundation entitled, "Turning Dreams Into Success" by Bunny and Larry Holman.

Over the years Tom has written several scripts for the stage, commercial ventures and special events. He has also written stories, poetry and parody song lyrics for various presentations. In addition to "'Twas The Night Before Christ" he has also published, "Santa's Prayer" – 100% of the proceeds from both books benefit the Children's Home Society of South Dakota.

Tom's involvement with Children's Home Society began in 1992 when he was asked if he would volunteer to play Santa Claus for the kids during a Christmas party. *"That experience made an impression on me that continues to move me even today. Here were these beautiful young souls who are struggling to overcome their tragic circumstances just so they can learn to feel safe and have someone value them, accept them . . . and to love them unconditionally. You only need to meet these kids for a short while and before you know it, they latch on to your heart."*

STEVE HOFFMAN
Graphic Designer / Illustrator

Steve Hoffman was born in Slayton, Minnesota. When he was two his family moved to Luverne, Minnesota where he grew up and went to school. He attended college at Alexandria, Minnesota and earned an Associate of Arts Degree.

In 1980, Steve and his wife Terri were married and moved to Sioux Falls. Terri works for Fiserv. They have two children. Their son, Ryan, is employed in drafting and construction services and married to Megan. They have a two year old son, Jackson, and live in Brandon, SD. Their daughter, Dana, is a senior at Hamline University in St. Paul, MN.

Steve worked at KSFY-TV for three years as their Art Director. In 1983, he joined the staff at Media One Advertising/Marketing and served as their Art Director for 14 years.

During his career, Steve has received numerous Addy's Awards for his work and is recognized among his peers as a proficient professional. In 2002, Steve received the American Advertising Federation's Silver Medal Award for his outstanding contributions to the advertising community.

In his spare time Steve enjoys golfing, photography, fishing, spending time with his grandson and restoring vintage cars. Over the years he has been an active volunteer with the South Dakota Advertising Federation as well as several other organizations in Sioux Falls.

'Twas The Night Before Christ is one of Steve's first experiences in illustrating a book of this nature. He has chosen to create this work using pastels to give his images a soft look yet with bright and vivid colors.

Special Thanks to the contributors who made this book possible:

ARTISTIC CONTRIBUTIONS

Written by Tom Roberts

Illustrated by Steve Hoffman

Project Coordination by Tammy Roberts

Photography by Henkin-Schultz Inc.

Printing by Sisson Printing, Inc.

CONTRIBUTIONS

JDS Industries

Midwest Editions

Rude Transportation Co.

'Twas the Night Before Christ
READER'S LOG

DATE_____   NAME OF READER_____

SPECIAL MEMORY_____

_____

"Christmas is for children . . . the child within us all.
It can stir that youthful, joyous spirit deep inside and renew our faith in humanity."

– Tom Roberts

DATE_____   NAME OF READER_____

SPECIAL MEMORY_____

_____

"Happy Christmas to all, and to all a goodnight!"

– Clement Clarke Moore

DATE_____   NAME OF READER_____

SPECIAL MEMORY_____

_____

"I will honor Christmas in my heart, and try to keep it all the year!"

(A Christmas Carol) – Charles Dickens

DATE_____   NAME OF READER_____

SPECIAL MEMORY_____

_____

"And the angel said unto them, "Fear not: for, behold, I bring you good tidings of great joy, which shall
be to all people. For unto you is born this day in the city of David a Savior, which is Christ the Lord."

– The Bible

DATE_____   NAME OF READER_____

SPECIAL MEMORY_____

_____

"Christmas is for the innocent . . . we're as innocent as they come!" (Snoopy and Woodstock)

– Charles Schulz

DATE_____   NAME OF READER_____

SPECIAL MEMORY_____

_____

"God rest you merry, Innocents, While Innocence endures.
A sweeter Christmas than we to ours, May you bequeath you yours."   – Ogden Nash

DATE_____   NAME OF READER_____

SPECIAL MEMORY_____

_____

"Joy to the world! The Lord is come; Let earth receive her King;
Let every heart prepare Him room, and heaven and nature sing!"   – Isaac Watts